This book is dedicated to my children - Mikey, Kobe, and Jojo.

Copyright © 2022 Grow Grit Press LLC. All rights reserved. No part of this book may be reproduced in any form without permission in writing from the publisher. Please send bulk order requests to growgritpress@gmail.com

Paperback ISBN: 978-1-63731-422-7
Hardcover ISBN: 978-1-63731-424-1

Printed and bound in the USA.
NinjaLifeHacks.tv

Ninja Life Hacks®
by Mary Nhin

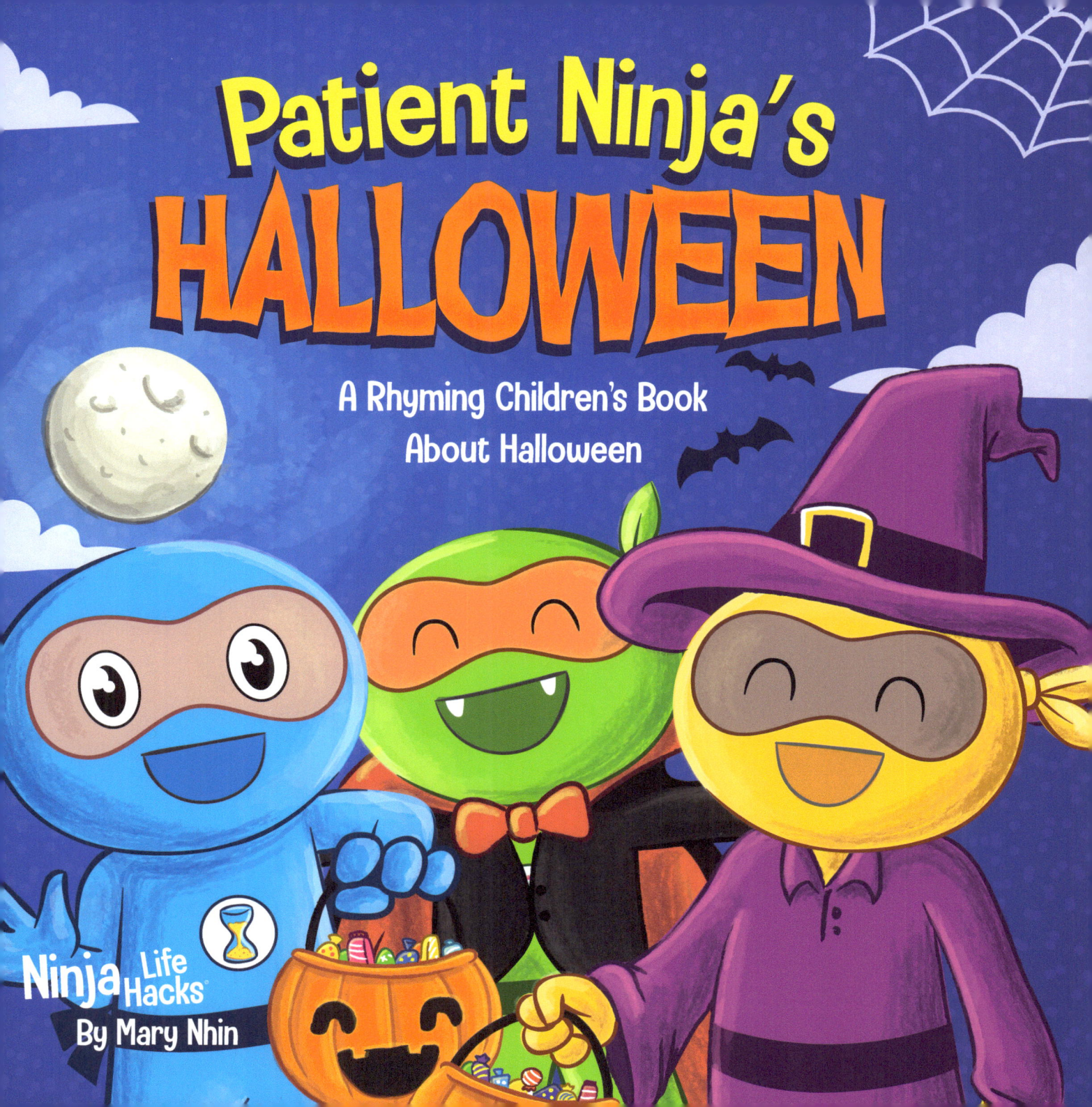

The other ninjas run outside,
A fancy-dress costume in hand.
And when I get in the door,
There's nothing left on the stand.

I try to shop at the second-hand store,
But that is empty as well.
So I try all the other stores nearby,
But **no one** has costumes to sell!

Looking at all the other ninjas,
Dressed up from head to toe.
There's one costume that no one's wearing,
So there's only one way to go.

What I have realized,
With no costumes left on the shelf,
Is that sometimes the best way to stand out
Is simply by being yourself!

www.ingramcontent.com/pod-product-compliance
Lightning Source LLC
Chambersburg PA
CBHW041106070526
44583CB00002B/80